Other poetry collection
by Cate McNider:

<u>Separation and Return</u>

is a collection of missives from the buried self in search of expression and communication to the conscious mind. These are poetic explorations, celebrations, and observations: of nature love, justice, and the mysteries that surround, confound and inform the soul; the product of a series of relationships beginning in her early twenties, which, she says, "sparked my curiosity for exploring my gifts. Childhood events created a buried treasure, which the arts helped me to explore, specifically, '[the] contents and whereabouts of my body/mind/soul.'" In her words the poetic effusions contained within these pages "cover a range of experience, from the separation of myself from myself in the process of healing and observations along the way, then returned to myself whole and healthy. The axiom 'healer heal thyself' applied to me long before I knew what it really entailed.

Here is a unique new poetic voice that is straightforward in tone, emotionally honest in expression, perceptive, unsentimental, and very powerful.

Visit **catemcnider.net** to buy your copy today!

ESCAPE VELOCITY

Cate McNider

atmosphere press

Dedicated to Ananda

Contents

Introduction

You enter a dark room, and what do you reach for first? The light switch, right?

The poems in this collection are single lights in a chronological string of them, to reflect and illuminate what is within you, a mirror — a poetic journey of my experience.

We are more alike than you may think, just as vulnerable and not knowing what to do at any moment, until we are faced with it. These poems are encounters with the moment in a dissolving and deepening process of letting go of *what I thought I knew*. An uncovering to see what *truly is*.

These are breadcrumbs along a birthright's journey to come to understanding of oneself and allow all the clothing of what we assume of reality to fall off and see ourselves nakedly, as lovingly embracing as the dreams we enter each night, whether we recall them in the morning or not.

What does all this mean that I am trying to prepare you to receive? If you go into a movie theater and it's a 3D movie, they give you glasses, so you can experience it literally, more fully, in depth. I am attempting to give you the glasses with which to read, to position you to understand each moment, what the moment *itself* is conveying to me, and thus crafted poetically to be assembled into this collection.

The reason for our being in separate bodies in the first place is for the Creator to see and experience itself in the myriad and multiples of experiences and grow and expand in consciousness from that 3D movie. An endless gallery of deeper and deeper understanding. You are reading *you* in these pages, perhaps not where you are just yet, but something you've felt before perhaps, strangely, in a walk alone on the beach, in a lover's eyes, or in the rejection of a gift you wanted to give, but it was not accepted. What is underneath, waiting to be re-cognized?

So this is my invitation, a ticket as it were to enter into the Theater of the Void, to turn on the light within you, to close your two eyes to the illusionary demands of the 'world' and encounter the lush and wondrous being-ness that waits within you. It's never what you think it is, and the discovery of that will lead to moments of those mini-lights being turned on within *you*.

The want of any mother is for their child to learn and grow and be alright, and many times, it's not that, it's dark and painful and things you can't wrap your brain around — understanding how, for example, something could hurt you so deeply and it be called *Love*. That is the journey of one's birthing oneself into realizations of higher and higher dimensions of understanding and compassion, to come so far as to have not left at all, to enter and embrace *all that is,* **the way it is.**

And so like the heartbeat of the mother, I hope you feel the pulse of *love* in the flow that is sometimes an ocean, other times a torrent of a river, the calm of a lake, a trickle of a mountain brook, or passing through the river Styx to the other side.

You will find the language I use, and the way I use it to represent the actual experience of which the poem relates. You will find repetition of the use itself, to refer to *its* **actuality**, which is not an idea, but a lived experience, a Truth. I mean what I say, as you will see, often bluntly with humor and again with *love*.

This collection is a window into the stripping away of illusions, conditioning and habits, and societal expectations and identity, to reveal the beauty of *what is* underneath everything we've been taught to believe, and how in order to understand where we've arrived as a baby, to assume the clothing of the environment in order to survive, there comes a time when that is exactly what one is called to do. The depth of the pain is equal to the height of the rising *potential*, that is the **Escape Velocity** needed [to realize one's Self].

This is the journey, if you are ready for that lifetime of uncovering and letting go of *what you think you know*, to open yourself, and if this is not that lifetime for you, then these are bread crumbs for you when you are ready, so when you do encounter a similar feeling moment, it may trigger a light to go on. Then this book will have met its purpose, to inspire courage, to keep investigating, to know it's all-ready inside you, and it's only going to be *you* that does it for **you.**

This is the kind of language you can expect; the emphasis with italics and dashes, and positioning of words to express an actual, real experience. The language used, the way I use it is letting *it* speak from the experience, as best as words can deliver. The organization of the concept and words may be an interruption of how you may have thought about a subject before; jostling and disorienting you, to break up some way you thought things were, or how you previously perceived them.

Take your time reading them, let it sink in — allow a new experience. I hope this opens pages in the volumes waiting within you.

~ Cate McNider

Happiness

I want to be as soft as you,
as solid and as fluid —
as knowing and as being in the present;
simultaneously not there at all,
except as a wave and a particle.

Whale's Song

If only I could insert my self,
angiogram balloon
inside your arteries, open you,
let the moon's tide take the pain
way out to sea —
let the whales song
cradle your soul back into love.

The End of War

The end of war is like the beginning of war;

cherry trees blossom,

                        then drop their petals,
        another is soon to follow,

it takes the breath away.

The Void

The Void swallowed me.
Up it went over my head:
Blackness, calm and peace.
I recognized my Self *in it*.
It is what *i am*.
I did not die,
i live in it.

Sans Eyes

Imagine *feeling* as your primary sense,
what is within you
giving directive.
It is dark, there is no need for eyes,
because all is *felt*.
All is
within you.
What do you *f e e l*?

Evanescence

The eyes and rest of the senses
are instruments of this reality.
The only sense that crosses all
dimensions is *feeling*.
They arrive as waves, the message
bared as the frequency.
Feeling passes through us,
if we,
a silent net,
allow it to present itself to us, purely.
Its only apparatus of expression
is experiencing it in our whole self
and understanding *its message*, untainted.
Eyes are to see physical reality, and even then
our eyes are not true to what *is* true
and often cannot be trusted.
The eyes see what they want to see mostly,
through the filter of the mind,
not what exactly is before them.
The illusion's clevernesses are our own,
and of our own making.

Consensual

All is moving inside me,
allowing the flow of Nature's power,
our consensual power, to exist.
Dark night covers my being,
I wake in deep space; the long arm
of the milky way comes from my back.
I am a dancing frog in the rainforest.
I am the swelling heat of summer.
I feel the waving wheat of the Great Plains.
I smell the soft air after a summer's rain,
somewhere. I hear a bell far off,
and then it happens —
letting myself *be done*.

It Takes Very Little

It takes very little for the mind to construct a story;
a scent, a meeting, a transfer of property
and it has travelled ten thousand miles
in search of a conclusion, that was also constructed
around another fanciful arrangement of circumstances
that originated in a misunderstanding which
fled the premises in search of a place to hide.
Thereby for the sake of Truth, was the death
of the hiding place, and the story awoke to find
itself unraveled into nothingness.

Because I See It

Because I see it, *it* changes
before my eyes,
the landscape morphs,
the meaning in the symbols.
What am I saying to myself?
The feeling cloaks itself into
a narrative, it's all in code,
shapes, colors, characters
to tell me something
to show myself who I am,
what is possible, what is within.
What speaks to me in feeling,
my mind reads the code
and re-works it into a story,
tells me, I am the creator
dreaming my life into being.
Prescience at dawn, wakes me
to pee, to go back again to the inner
film to see how it turns out,
non-sequiturs pasting
themselves in a patch-worked
morse code, art of the highest order,
illusive, un-boundaried, fluid
communication: itself with *itself*.
I record it when I have to get up,
journalist of the *collective* mind.
I don't know what it means, except
when it reveals *itself*.
It has the power to shade its
illumination, should I be looking for
it to make logical sense in this reality.

What am I not?

What am I not I am not not everything everything is in me and
I am you and you are me and everything runs through this
body, this river of consciousness, these dreams and reality
is our other dreams in all the reality is, what am I not but
everything. And so everything moves through me and if I am
not not everything I have no need for identifying as anything
but what I am. I am not not everything. I am not not everything
everything runs through me and so I am not any one thing,
I am everything. I don't need to identify with something or
not identify with something out of this know that the both
and neither are true. I am not not everything. I am not not
everything I am the space through which everything runs
through which everything comes I am that feeling that there is
no word for or words for. I am not not everything. I am not not
my sister I am not not my friend I am not not my enemy, I am
not not the villain. I am not not everything I am what it is, it is
what I am whatever that is.

Blue Marble

One is.
All the clothing, habits and identifications
distance (you):
rainbow chasing gets you no closer to seeing
what *is*, (does).
Opposite is always true, defy (your mind).
The world is not responsible for (loving) you.
It owes you no-thing, unless you love
yourself some-thing.
The world is a divine looking-glass of your
(own) distorted creation, twisted thought
comes out tense, wrought with worry —
don't trust the cover story,
all lies (like fleas) need hosting.
Definition (runs) in the family,
too limiting and costly —
take class, sex, religion and race
to the laundry, wash its mouth with soap.
Stripping (oneself) naked is the safest
choice yet, under the blue tent sky,
ball of rock, spinning, in atomic soup —
No-thing is going to get you every-where-ness.

Lay With Me

When I invited Death to lay with me
and keep me company, I felt my next
breath in its entrance, sweet
like a desert flower, the wind
blowing through a garden of succulents.

She got real close and pain of loss
dissolved. She took residence
inside, her place within me
waiting. Her presence strengthened me,
giving me cause to strip all away I do not need:
judgement, fear, illusion.

I felt her inside me, where she had
always been, my ally, my best friend —
matching my life with her counter self
we two together made one door,
one window, either side saw the other
perspective and was balanced.

Life Raft

Form is the life raft
of the mind
in a sea of terror —
emptiness.

Tension

The mind is a muscle
too often in flexion.

Mother God

Mother God in all her silent deep pillowy
emptiness holds the space for all her children
to learn and grow, using whatever
they've come to mis-understand, returning
countless times, spinning countless timelines
of centuries, epochs and myths to awaken
to the Truth that's been waiting
inside them all this time.

A Lie

Our lives, not a linear reality.
A lie is a lie no matter how many times
you repeat it.
My fathers worn out anger on my sleeve
never felt right and my mother's silence
didn't save me.
I don't know who she was.
Pretending is a child's game that
gets monetized and mercy is the grave.

You can think yourself small, a lie
is a lie no matter how many times
you make it sound appealing.
The world prays itself to sleep with lies;
commemorates them into sculpture,
while Truth is always right in front of you.
A lie is a lie no matter how many
ways you color it.

Shadow World

Living on earth is a second hand store;
this shadow world can never satisfy
Spirit's truth for which this dream reality
is provided, for us to transcend.
What we think we want, looks like,
isn't what we want at all.
It isn't here.
It isn't any-*where*.
It's inside us.
When we chase and live the symbol,
it passes as a chimera, paining
and disappointing us and those we love,
knotting us in the process.
When those ties are loosened and
you feel your immensity,
awe strikes
and nothing is again, as it was.
You live as the witness you were
meant to, not taking any-thing
too seriously.

Growing

When a poet grows beyond words, she paints.
When she grows beyond painting, she walks
and smells and sees and tastes and touches
the wind that she knows to be *herself*.

Salute to the Sentry

Spinous passage of lightning carries the message
up, beyond my form's lineage, distilled through
rice paper layers of brain into the ethers, cranium
opened to receive the blue lit moon.
Pinwheels of color spin, projected by my eye
whatever they touch, that the reality of things
is broken down in its snaking rainbow, such
is the price of reverie.
Primordial waves, personified in moving color,
dance about my vision's periphery, revealing
the lying nature of the brain's perception.
What else can turn a grey porous soup to a
kaleidoscope of form and senses to experience
them; the brain — the sentry of the realms.

Tao of Movement

Why things remain the same
even as they change, is the work
of two hands, the Tao of movement.
Why the names change and history
repeats itself is because this is *what it is*,
a cosmic washing machine — the stains
keep coming and some are very stubborn!

To believe you have only one life is a thought
of guppies — you wish you didn't have to resolve
the consequences of your misunderstood actions!
No, no my friends, your immensity of *all that is*,
beckons every moment of every moment.

As if one lifetime, in one timeline was the
journey of your infinity — are you a gnat?!
Come alive and realize what you are,
God itself.

Driving Through Memories

All that wanting,
all that pain from losing,
all for an idea
from somewhere
that no longer holds matter;
they are just landmarks.
What I loved was the feeling
that *I* made into a **thing**.
The feeling was *in* me.
The feeling was in *me*.

Elegance

The movement of all things:
the planets, space itself,
the stars, elements themselves
within me and without,
defined *itself* as the *allowing*
of all to be itself,
is itself, elegance.
Its wholeness is dependable.

Working Theory

Faith and trust are a working theory;
the unknown that holds a place,
where an experience has yet
to replace the words.

Dream Dissolution

Peeling wallpaper,
distinct sense of time eroding
water-stained walls,
four corners morphed into
a point of perspective.
People coming in and walking
around uninvited:
I told them to go!
I wanted some coffee, but
decided not to go out.
Single hot plate.
I asked the landlord to change
the two flimsy plywood doors,
he smiled with no intention.
I kept telling people to leave:
(thoughts personified). I could
see a guy on the floor below
in a bathtub, submerged in ice.

Poetry Is

Poetry is an experience that is put
into a form — existence is poetic;
it is not separate from what is — the
experience of *what is*, is poetry.

Amidst the Doing

Amidst the doing of things for my work,
there is a calling to myself, an awareness,
a presence of my larger self, of *all that is*,
a feeling, a vibration, that carries this
message, that is passing through me.
And these things I do, to 'make a living'
are small, though not without consequence,
to the presence of *what is*, which
is mostly *felt* in this darkened world.
This is perspective showing me
itself.

Media Lens

The 'war against this',
the 'fight against that'...
Stop it!
Recognize the war
is *in YOU*, and
leave the world out of it.

Decision

A decision made
is a question answered,
is a direction eliminated,
is the self revealed.

Not Just

Poetry is not just pretty turns
of phrases, angry rants
or metaphors and rhymes;
its purest active form,
is the pursuit of Truth within,
distilling oneself to the essence.
...and if need be,
letting *It* flow upon the page.

Changing Timelines

We are none of us the same from day to day,
unless we fix ourself to the lie of linear reality
and then... something will always come
and knock you
off the ledge,
like a cat to a cup — the floor beckons
and the cup is in pieces!
Now, you really have something to do: stay broken
or throw away *what you think you know*.

Crossroads in the Garden of Being

A flower cannot be rushed
to blossom; leave it to the sun,
the soil and the rain,
to realize it already has.

Truth Is

Truth is neither cold nor hard, but that
you make *your* self so, in the ignoring of it.

Truth cares not what you think.
Truth cares not what you want.
Truth *is*.
It will dissolve the illusions and lies
one constructed, albeit painfully, if you resist.
Allow it into you, it will show you *its* beauty.

Truth is neither cold nor hard, but that
you make *your* self so, in the ignoring of it.

Labels

Labels confine, taking you down
wrong roads, decades to undo.
I am but a vibrational frequency —
now you see me, *now you don't.*

Walking Up Third Avenue

The wind speaks to me
in its language:
velvet, ravenous,
torrid, tempestuous.
This time it opened a door inside,
summoned a peace in me,
to my solar plexus,
an inner calling, eyes closed
allowed entry to the Void.
I never want it to dissolve,
or be distracted —
a lover whose kisses make
you tremble
at the power of their softness.

Sitting

A feeling of being
filled up
from within,
with space,
such that the space
outside of me and
within me was
indistinguishable.
Persona disappeared
and I was one
with that singular
vibration.
I was vibration
itself.

The Point

The art is not the object.
The making of the art,
is not the object.
Even the process of making
the art is not the object.
It is what the art is
c o m m u n i c a t i n g
that is the point, from
where it comes, that is
the object.
The painting itself has
no value, except to enjoy;
how does it make you feel?
Look to the source for
the message, it's in the
source.
It is a message to itself,
it gives of itself to itself.
The experience is the art.
Understanding where it
comes from is the art.
Allowing it is the art.
Accepting it is the art.
Knowledge of this, is
the point.

Best People

I meet all the best people
in obituaries and am instantly

saddened, I really would have
loved to talk with that person!

Known them. I feel at a loss,
I missed meeting such an interesting,

accomplished and much loved human
being. There are no assholes that die,

or sons of bitches that made their
children's lives a living hell —

all that is in the 'omituaries.'

The G A P

Accepting the g a p between us
is the hardest thing, when I want to
share with you, what it is *I* mean.
I see you don't recognize me, I've changed
so much, and when I tell you "It's me"
you gasp and clutch your heart,
"You cut your hair or have you lost weight?"
"No, I stopped pretending this body is who I am."
"It's ok, you'd have to have let go too, to understand
I am all around, the wind, the rain, the waves in the air.
I am not confined to a single body."
This conversation is on the page because
I cannot say it to your face: "This is a dream
and you are a thought in the mind of Infinity."

Keyhole

Right now you're looking
through a keyhole;
you will describe the room
from that tiny aperture, but
if you unlock the door, open it
and walk through it,
the room
will show *itself*
to you.

Un-borned and Real-ized

I felt myself undifferentiated,
a marrow cell in the all
of the no-thingness,
hyperventilating darkness,
spewing sand,
spat upon a wilderness.
I am the creator of worlds
and the destroyer of worlds.
The thinker
of the thought of myself — myself just a
thought, a blip on the mass of Godliness.
I am new — unborned.
Un-born of woman, but born of myself
—untainted, awakened
as a thought is real-ized, made real,
my wings spread, exhaling heat,
consuming the air, shaping
my world with my wings.
A sphere of yellow-orange light
rose from this belly,
and I was born of this rising, new,
being conceived in the exhaling breath of
fierceness of power —
Do Not
mistake
me
for anything
you
know.

Allowance

Life lived in allowance
is a different sort of life.
It's receptive — a flower
waiting for the honeybee,
the right egg waiting
for the right sperm
to create the household
for another spirit
to take up residence.

It's a kind of inside-out strength,
the absolute absence of
muscle, but it works like
a muscle in the non-doing.
This allowing, this acceptance,
this arriving into form, in its
right time to show *itself*,
brings a smoothness of being.

It is a kind of knowing —
a mother who feels the movement
of the child within her, turning
and kicking, though it's not fully
formed or ready to be born,
she *knows* it is coming.

When it's birthed, it never looks
as you imagined, but still,
you took action, nurtured its becoming,
and it's
what it is.
Always what *it is*.

Recourse

When the outside hasn't
noticed you, either in neglect
or isolation, there is
nowhere else to turn,
but to go within oneself.

Perhaps that is the precise
reason for it,
as if one has plotted
before birth to put oneself
on such a course
as to *have* to discover
this inverse pathway
out of pain and suffering.

Whether you believe or
can conceive of so called
'reincarnation' or multiple
timelines of existence,
if you find yourself going
in, it is because *it's time*!

Letting go of what you
thought you knew is an
unburdening, a relief.
The undoing of lies
is the beginning of
the road home.

Experience

Look into what you can't see,
feel what you can't touch,
taste what you can't smell —
it's now.

Playground

There was a sweet moment today
on the playground —
facing the sun, soaking up its
information, when I heard the children
coming into the playground, one by one,
about five or six of them, giggling and
playing together with their squeaky
voices, and then...
I was one of them again — inside.
I remember the glee and freedom from
responsibility, to climb and fall,
run and skip, be pushed down and fall over,
laugh about it, and get up and do it again.
The mother's faces looked stern and
protective. I was invisible, sitting facing
the sun, under cover of sunglasses,
but my ears wide open to sound of time —
inside.

From the Stillness Comes

Let the energy play you.
You are after all, Its instrument.
You are Its form,
making Its sound
blowing through
Its reed —
your whole being is shaped
by Its movement,
let It show *Itself* to you.

I Am One of You

For those seekers who look within
for real answers take heart, bigger

questions will lead you to unexpected places,
where you could not have imagined. Be

not envious of those who have asked superficial
questions, not challenging their assumptions

or habits, who *appear* to have more than you,
for their derivatives will not take them

to the unknown, or to the revealing. Not
everyone wants to *know* what you want

to know from experience, from your soma,
not from your mind.

Birthday — Times Around the Sun

I am not forgotten, to myself.
I remember many knee scrapes,
rejections and ignorances of others,
as I look upon the healed scars.
It is only I, that recognize the markers along
my journey and more importantly:
the undoing and undressing of the mask
and inner tensions built, in order to survive.

Now, going forward, it is the *absence* of it
that allows naked feelings to spontaneously
announce themselves, dance within my being,
whispering the whys of lessons my Self
taught me, and that revealing the *original*
nature of my Self, *is* the way home.

Lush Landscapes

My eyes need to be fed: trees,
river, mountain, shore of sky,
as Metro North jostles up
the Hudson line.
The absence of jarring towers
enclosing the heavens,
the curtain of green soothes my brain;
their verdant waves come to synchronize
with the river's lapping.

The friend I'm traveling to visit owes
me a favor, I'm calling in the marker.
I envision to be able, one day, to call
the valley shores my home.

Man on Earth — In Cooperation

Man is man.
He sells out his brother,
no matter the color or class.
His victim isn't special;
it's just what he does.
You may not remember, but
last time, you were the one
doing the betraying.
Now, you get to experience
the other side of the equation.
Understand the cooperation
of light and dark in order for
the whole thing to rise, and
morality isn't necessary, because
conscience has been awakened —
Truth takes care of *itself*.

9/11 Anniversary

We sat in the crowded
back room of the church, waiting
to hear poetry take us out of our miseries;
our programs, barely moving
the stagnant humid air,
flapping butterfly wings,
randomly lighting on twigs this September night,
that downtown, eighteen years ago portended the end
of another era, and the beginning
of surveilled atrocities and a war
that has no end.

She Who Is

I inhabit this body now.
I saw from my body — my whole
body sees.
The energy passing through, opened
a perception called 'seeing.'
It is not eyes as the orbs, but a vibration.
Right now I feel not my name — which
is why I would say right now, I feel different
than her, how she *has* felt.

She who was, has accepted me, who is,
in,
to be.
It is me.
I am the stream that runs through this body.

Crusader and Geisha — The Painting

His tightened edges have softened.
There is a glow beneath the weight
he still appears to carry, or so it seems,
by the graying that frames his face.
She brought such movement into his
life, because he asked for it, not
exactly *how* she dug up his ghosts
but *that* she called them out to be freed.

It was not easy for him, that she was such
a miner of her own as well as his,
but he didn't mind the frequent sex
that punctuated the coaxing out of his
stubbornness, soothing his insecurities,
or celebrating with an afternoon
of painting together.

The nights he got her through the lawsuit,
by drawing together at his kitchen table
were the sweetest and best therapy
anyone ever bestowed upon her; the angst
of betrayal's repetition was combed out in
the uncertain lines of charcoal overlaying
colors of watery transparency.
She thanks him for that.

She misses it, but she will not stir his
present with the past, now,
he has his own version.
Hers is still tangy with the memory
of enticing him with healing and being
transformed by gentle, sometimes quick
strokes of his brush upon her canvas.

I Have Always Been Myself

I have always been myself,
there is no hiding, no lies,
no need for fear or anxiety,
only what my Spirit drives me
toward: my future.
But I do know, whatever *it is*,
will return to my original, sans
the costume of form,
a quivering vibration:
contracts paid,
message delivered.
Body, no body,
I will always be myself,
however I choose to adorn it,
a signature of the sacred
singularity.

Prison Mind

I see the prison of the mind, how
the habit of letting it guard and dictate
keeps me shuffling, legs chained
to invisible rules I rebelled against
decades ago.
Or so I thought I had sloughed them off,
but eliminating the anchors of it in the
body has loosened its grasp, and so it
now works even harder not to lose its
employment.

It must be done softly, under its radar,
which is near to impossible, but not to
take hold in the first place, one has to
become aware that one *is* taking hold,
letting it run through, over and over
infecting and distorting the body.
The life force has to be allowed to *flow*.

Letting one *let oneself alone* takes great
focus and discipline; being captured and
freeing oneself again. Slipping under the mind
stealthily, takes decades of practice, perseverance.
The body's senses help in diverting attention
to its childlike hunger for attention; always
pulling on you, 'mommy look at me, look at me!'

Regaining one's witness is wresting an opioid
from a junkie, making the separation for good,
allowing the space, to see the Void, experience
emptiness and know it is the ground for listening
truly: to let oneself *be*.

Things I Tell Myself

Things I tell myself aren't easy to hear
but I know they're true — *I know*. When

I accept them, it gets easier. I tell myself
'you're all you have' and it's true. That's

so for all of us, but we claim possession
of people which can't be possessed, but

we tell ourselves we 'have' them. Things
are easier to possess, and even they go

missing, fall apart and return to their
makers. I tell myself, I'm responsible for

it all. I accept, and my body unwinds
another guy wire of tension attached

to another and another, until I'm too tired
to sit anymore and my eyes open.

Things I tell myself, I hear differently
now that there's more space inside.

I don't have to think in words anymore,
and no-thingness is good. I think they

call that *peace*, that do know it.

Watching

When I felt the me of me,
there was nothing,
emptiness,
but space.
Who was watching?
Yeah, who *was* watching?
Space with its ears and eyes,
its knowingness in its waves, pulsing.
Its pulse is my pulse,
no matter the skin
in between.

Chaos

Chaos is Man's idea of what
they can't see beyond.
It only looks like mayhem when
you don't know the source or the
function of the wave's message.
There is organization in all things;
The Law is a template, a mold,
out of whose order *all* things are created.
From the smallest atom to the vastness
of solar systems billions of miles from
heliocentric earth, there is a sameness
and a relationship in all forms.
Look at the body — its magnificent
organization, and when things go awry,
it's because the mind has distorted or misused it.
There is a natural twist, a tension, that keeps
us tethered in our reality, then add layers
of fears of what you don't know,
and the light can't get through the knots!
Also, metaphor would never work if there
wasn't a sameness at all levels.
Behind every curtain of myth is its origin;
peek behind the tinted blinds of your eyes
and recognize them looking back at you!

You Matter

Before he became my love,
laying atop him, clothed,
looking at each other,
he said: "You matter."
It was a stunning statement, a
stinging of grace, a moment my
heart was pierced by the Truth of Love.

That was a key that turned a lock
that opened a door inside me,
where no one else had the capacity
or lack of narcissistic agenda to affect
such an impact of opening myself to
trust this messenger of love.

It shattered the perception, that previous acts
of repeated betrayal and misuse had imprinted
countless experiences that I did not, in fact,
matter, as a person, but had predominantly
been shown treatment as an object
for someone else's satisfaction,
pending their approval.

I was experiencing something different,
a statement that broke with past messages.
I don't remember if I teared up or cried,
I was so disarmed, my pain arrested,
cauterized, and my curiosity piqued
by a man who spoke my heart.

Shiny Trinkets

The nature of mind itself is tyranny — a crow
pecking and scraping the invisible space we all share,

for shiny trinkets; tinsel, paper clips, collecting souvenirs.
It caws across the din of the multitude, proud of its possessions

blinding us, unaware that thoughts have mass freely speeding
through the soup of primordial waves — their thoughts are *felt*,

a signature tug intruding through my sky, when I'm doing some-
thing else, but the thoughts travel on. I don't take hold, and I let

it go on. The mind is not contained only within the walls of each
skull, the sky is fluid and our lightning thoughts pierce the dark

and stormy, until one day the cord breaks, no signal goes out.

Jolly Tickle — Quarantined Too Long

So, I'm getting the hang of this Dickinson,
its pretty jaggeds and straws.
I've gotten it engined, it's doing its own
real estate or without too much needle.
I did my morning diner three times and my
can't look went reefer and reefer.
This is waking up my surgeon sensation and
rigging my anomalies.
Now everything is getting blendered.
I hear the pigeons across the way basketing and cribbing.
It tickles my champagne and my scalpel relaxes.
Beard of the Trees — Now I'm getting somewhere
deep in the leaves.
My mind still gavels to regain dictator, it placates me
"out of order" — It's quite white shirt and no. 2 pencils.
Last night's sand felt so good — I wish the velvet corseted.
Why does raking this remind me so much of biscuits literature?
Too many things that don't make dollars, make pounds
and this makes more ballpoint pen than any of them!
Where does one plunder after this?
I wish I could Stargate to My Front Porch-land right now, walk
though the marys and see the exploding alien sky!

Black Is a Feeling

Black is a feeling, not a color. It absorbs
all vibrations, and white wavelength reflects all.

Looking outside of yourself for unity,
will fall short of what you really want to feel,

absolutely. Hope for the discovery of yourself,
therein, and you will unearth the lies and illusions.

I can *feel* it all within me, and accept it all
within me. This is unity, *inside*.

Small Is Mighty — Sculptors of Reality

You may *feel* small in this great Universe,
so you create an ego, but the irony is

IT'S all inside *YOU* — accountable to you
and you accountable to it. Affecting an

outcome is determined by your feeling,
and the energy you give an action, as to how

and what it turns out to be. That is great
responsibility. Atoms and molecules,

messengers of magnetism, soldiers of form,
heroes that answer the call of becoming some-thing

know this — why don't we? This poem for example,
is an assemblage of a thought, culled from the ethers,

laid out, inked in lines of symbols pointing
to something *that is*, in essence *itself*, that *was* before

I put pen to paper, invisible — the recognition of peace
passing through my being.

Un-tethered-ness

A day of intense un-tethered-ness, to anything —
feeling the echo of previous years' habit

of doing, doing so much — as those movements
bounce back to me in the Cosmic Canyon, they

resemble the activity's memory, and each
hearing is further and further away, dimly felt,

as a baby's reflex upon which all other movement
is built. It's there underneath and lets me get

out of bed, walk to make coffee and sit to feel
what to do. And when nothing calls me: the mechanism,

still trying to do its job, fails, a lumber saw with no
trees to cut, the forest bare — no appointments made,

social obligations gone, I feel the spaciousness
that was always covered up. To exist purely

as one is oneself, is enough, has to be
because here I am, untethered — belonging to it all.

Grey Becomes Matter

Transitioning from one reality to another,
night dreams back to here, I see the waves

that my brain transforms into what we see
and live in. This morning's waves were long

and blobby, like a lateral lava lamp, grouping
with other blobs, lengthening and stretching

until they were all processed by my brain. Gone
were the grey globs into the grey matter. That's

no mistake, probably somewhere the scientists
know grey makes grey matter grey, until the rods

and the cones splash on the color and the occipital
department of life says, 'Yes!' This is where Dorothy

landed, and magic happens, where wicked witches'
shoes become the transport of destiny that she has

to face trial after trial and ally after ally to realize
she was wearing Prada the whole time!

Open Day

An open day is always filled with possibility.
What will come? What epiphany will emerge

from released tension? I watched the day
unfold, tiredness setting in at teatime, enough,

Enough for a day. A call from within to sit.
I light a candle and a small stick of incense

to fragrance the air, to awaken my senses as I
go in, to feel what is calling me — to *listen*.

I hear a message from my left atrium,
"you can't know what you don't know".

The tension released, my mind eases its grip
to let me breathe deeper, allowing expansion

everywhere, feeling more spacious, the false
concept undone. My father's message to me when I

was eight, that *thinking* was superior to *feeling*,
made me abandon my own heart, like an electrical

power utility, it shut down that function until decades
later when I could handle the voltage. Never underestimate

the power of feeling, the power of blood and energy
and especially the space between them all.

What I'm Not

I know what I'm not,
that leaves *what is*, and that is
good enough for me.

Look No Further

Look no further than
your Self for change, it is
all inside you now.

Outlived The World

When you have outlived
the world, and its distractions,
you are dangerous.

Change In Me

Walking through the hood,
I saw the change in me,
and me not *in* it.

Invisible

Love is unseen and
everywhere, it is the
air we breathe — allow it.

Illusion's Ransom

It's yours, the pain is yours,
borrowed from the vat of human experience.

You've put your stamp on it, how you feel
about it, what it makes you think of,

not only death, but the vagaries of living
in a seamless container of flesh and fluids,

some that spill out, and others that fester
and boil, twist you into a tourniquet

and starve you of hope of ever getting past
the reasons for their becoming so time

consuming. We measure people by their
pain in bravery (or stupidity) for enduring it,

multiplying it, we think we have something
to prove, that by holding on, we will signal the absolute

devastation of one's spirit, and thereby prove
to ourselves that we really don't exist and extinguish

ourselves. But we do, whether in a sac of molecules
assembled or in a frequency transversing realities,

we exist. We exist to prove to ourselves
of the pain of existence, the loss of what

we wanted to believe, being the single most painful
and often the final illusion that strings together all the rest.

That then, the necklace loosened of its catch, the talismans
scatter and one can have peace, having let go of fantasy,

desperately trying to prove ourselves on the Mount Everest
climb of ego, shoving our boot in the faces of the other,

and thinking that things and status and money
are more important than the overall sensual experience,

wisdom gained, humility accepted and the question
you came here to have answered, is recognized.

Girl Child

She doesn't know the language of her sex yet,
as she stands in her crib eyeing the activity beyond

the rails. She can't wait to get out and talk
like she knows something. When she looks back

at the road she's walked and sometimes crawled
home bloody, she realizes all her mannerisms

were in *response*, they weren't hers, not even her
golden hair that she got from her mother, or the indigo

eyes she got from her father; everything
was handed down a long chain of time

kept in God's waistcoat. What was hers was
the gleam, the place she left to come here,

to feel what tender flesh she could wrap
around her idea of Life. Much of it stung

of what it wasn't to be and sang of Momma's
lullabies and tasted like pancakes, soaked with the

blood of trees. Strange world, she thinks as
she adapts, and gets lots of skinned knees,

her mind way ahead of her little legs racing
to get to class. The lessons learned in the wider

world, taught her the only way out was the way *in*.
And she wanted that camel ride home, and found

the oases weren't wet, but the Void *felt* inside her.
And then she remembered the pyramid and the dry nights

with fragranced winds kissing her brown skin
on the balcony overlooking the distance to the village

beyond. It was then, in the Now, that had been hers,
was *hers*, the essence was the same — the memory.

It was a call to follow, to allow *it* to lead her, to surrender
it all, to recognize what she already was:

an idea in the gleam of her own consciousness.

Process

To see what *It is*,
You have to see what It's not,
then you're free to live.

Undone

I have not *become*,
but undone all that was not
me — the conditions.

This Is That

I know you because
I know me, we are the same,
the rest is a dream.

How To Be Human

We've got it all wrong.
There's physical strength one cultivates
through exercise, and there's the strength
of the body that comes from the inner
communion with the *soul* and the workouts
that happens in the dream space. The inner
supports the outer instead of the outer
tension holding up the inner.

The body knows more than you think
it does, and speaks in its own way, but
only the outlier discovers this, quietly,
pursuing the journey of the spirit
through the realms and realities, seen
and unseen — mostly *felt*.

You wouldn't know it to see it, because
our eyes aren't trained for the wider
spectrum of perception; we're rewarded
instead, for the plundering and capture
of the weak, a narrow behavioral selection
leaning towards violence, crippling most,
which weakens the whole.

You might feel it in their presence, a steadiness
and curious loving detachment of the drama playing
out on the stage we call the world, they *know*
because they've experienced themselves as
the other — and know them not to be separate.

Slow The Frames

Long are the moments,
when I slow down and feel the
air *as* an ocean.

Peacemaker

A peacemaker doesn't get in the middle
where they don't belong.

Void's Eye View

I saw in my inner vision, an atomic explosion,
nuclear green, giant air fungus expanding,

a mushroom cloud, three weeks before Putin
brazenly bombed Ukraine It popped into my Void,

showing me itself, as *it is*, a possibility. The reality
exists, the question is, will we again step into that frame?

We are children playing with Laws of the Universe we
don't fully understand nor comprehend the consequences.

Do we really want to have all that is left of you be a shadow
on a wall burned into it as it was in Hiroshima?

Visions come *to us*, they cannot be forced, they come
as warnings, as an existent potential, showing us

what is already there, but do we *choose* it, like a card
out of a deck to become this reality? They come to many

who are open, who are seeking truth about the nature
of *All That Is*. They are messages from ourself to our Self.

Visions are different from imagination, though they come
through the same means — deeper, direct, often without

instruction, a stamp of an image or a moving scene,
a face unidentified out of time, or a shape in its becoming

something, as yet unfamiliar to the mind. Cassandra knew
and was not heard, WW2 happened not so long ago, whose

remaining generation is dying out, as another greedy
aggressor thrusts its tentacles, visions become postcards

of a future a few chess plays away from a dangerous outcome
we would all be forced to endure. Visions are classified

material, they come through *who* they come through
for *their* own reasons, messengers of the Void.

'Escape Velocity' Definition: in *celestial mechanics, escape speed* is the minimum speed needed for a free non pro-pelled object to *escape from the gravitational influence* of a primary body, thus *reaching an infinite distance from it.*

Ideal speed, ignoring the atmospheric friction.*

*wikipedia.org

Escape Velocity

If life is an hourglass, I'm in the narrow of the funnel,
going through an essential passage, the elimination

of the past, through the doorway of only what will fit
through: Truth, love, intelligence and the curiosity to keep

going. To keep allowing the particles of light to breakdown
what isn't real, to allow its essence to be what invisibly

settles at and fills the bottom, which then becomes the top, always
emptying. We all wish for the startle not to have happened,

the beating not to have happened, the abuse not to have happened.
This is the icy chasm of Everest climbers who must traverse

with clawed boots over ladders to extend across to the other side,
the acceptance of the conditions of the climb, the fog, the avalanche,

earthquake and aftershocks that re-freezes one in place at the event
horizon, the image remains, but you are gone. The greatest

of tribulations are the fuel needed for escape velocity, to propel
and launch one beyond past attachments, transcending insecurities,

fears, pains and disappointments, to keep allowing through *all*
that does not belong in the now; the practice is long, *the happening*

is a moment. The answers come...feelings are accepted
as the vibrational waves they truly are, passing through the vast Void

within, and like the climbers focused on the rungs and not the chasm
below, they cross safely, to the next and the next; that is the practice,

and can be the only 'thing' to 'hold onto' within one's Self. Focus on the curiosity, the love, and intelligence, breath entering and leaving,

allowing energy to move, the stroke of the paint brush on the canvas, the pen upon the paper, not the chasm of doubt, negativity and rejections

past. No one can see inside us but ourselves, and it is up to each, to look there, and the mountain's peak will show itself *within*;

the love is in the next step, is indeed what creates the next step — it is here that *what is*, is re-cognized.

"I'm Right Here," an experiential poem: Tap gently on your sternum rhythmically repeating the statement. Allow the tone and affect of the repetition and tapping to inform you each time, allow the changes to deepen, allow yourself to hear your Self, to bring you present to your body and self within it. Notice how your energy changes, allow it to flow, and any tears, or whatever, that may come with it.

I'm Right Here

I'm right here.
I'm right here.
I'm right here.
I'm right here.
I'm right here.
I'm right here.
I'm right here.
I'm right here.
I'm right here.
I'm right here.
I'm right here.
I'm right here.
I'm right here.
I'm right here.
I'm right here.
I'm right here.
I'm right here.
I'm right here.
I'm right here.
I'm right here.
I'm right here.
I'm right here.
I'm right here.
I'm right here.
I'm right here.
I'm right here.
I'm right here.
I'm right here.
I'm right here.
I'm right here.
I'm right here.

By Interior Design
or *Walk Across the Canyon*

We have no choice as infants, toddlers and then as children to *attach*
to our care takers, be they of blood or not, and our environmental

surroundings, cold, warm or temperate. That first moment of breath,
of sucking open the tree of life, the organ of interacting in this world,

happens, *'Ahh!'* with a cry or a gasp, testing its bellows, screaming
its way into this reality. Lungs, check; heartbeat, check; vocal cords,

check! And then what? *Not knowing* is the ground upon which
all attachments grow and lay their seeds into the fresh mind. And then

what? You don't know. Your body's needs speak for you, you don't
have language, but you're conscious. You feel but you don't have

words yet to attach to feelings, feeling is still pure, uncontaminated
by someone who tells you what it is, because someone did the same

to them. You feel. You feel the air. You feel your caretaker's moods,
their energy. New life wants to survive. You don't understand, so you

listen and hear. Will it affect your survival? That is the constant,
because you can't do for yourself yet. You don't even know that you

are asking that question, but you learn how crying is your question
and food or diaper change or love is the answer. *It* comes when you

cry. Attaching meaning to answers that come becomes the bedrock
of one's life. What you think it means is not necessarily true. These

become *invisible* habits upon which other habits build their visibility. And all identity habits follow and are then defended, possibly

to the death of someone because they *disagree*. The other is threatened, and it feels like their whole life is threatened when their identity

is questioned to those whose insecurity is strong. How are they not to meet conflict if everyone is attached to attachments?! They have

theirs, you have yours, and there is only so much land on this earth and only so many resources; wars are all a consequence of the arrival

on this planet, in this body, at this time. Belief that their attachment is more important than another's because they have more resources,

money, or influence, keeps the war going. They never cite themselves bearing their attachments as the *problem*. They never see themselves

as the source of the conflict. They can't see the way out of attachments and habits. Un-attachment brings freedom *within*. Detachment

from applying meaning allows the thing itself or the person to reveal itself. The *'ahh'* moment is a lived state of wonder and curiosity,

without the whole house of attachments crushing you. You just do, and accept and have no expectations of what will be; like a high wire

artist over the Grand Canyon, there is as much awareness of space inside that matches the outside, that balances you and you walk

towards the other side, to arrive where you came from; changed, evolved, experienced and having answered the question for which

you came — we are what we become, but
we don't always become what we are.

Blank Page

You're like freshly sunned laundry,
whose waves emanate messages, making sails

from the day's rhythmic breeze, thudding in its
captured tresses, beckoning to its fullness and shrinking

at the loss of the wind's power of movement
in a moment; the pattern will repeat itself

and you shall draw stresses to memories, like strings
pulled within you and we shall deliver whatever

you need, as we are endless, and open in our offering,
cycling the structures of the day from the well of being.

We, the waiting, voice this formlessness which you know deep
down inside, from which you come; what are you here to create?

Captivating Bling

No more accomplishments in the material world, *about*
the material world will ever again mean more than what

is within me, and what growth happens within me. I can
say goodbye to all that conditioned measurement of myself

with it. It bears no measure of me. There is no-thing
outside of me that can equal the growth within me.

The world does not decide who I am, I do. If it is
too busy with itself as *it is*, to recognize a member

of itself, it doesn't mean I am worth *less*, it just
means it can't recognize me because I'm not

playing its game anymore, I'm out. And it's
not some justification of rejections, but a recognition

that I have outgrown its limits, confines and costumes
to see the illusion for what *it is* — a dream to awaken from,

and move on. If I publish the poetry I've written since
2010, into a second collection, whatever happens

with it, if it is reviewed or bought, or put on bookstore
shelves, its purpose has already peaked inside me,

a shoehorn that expanded me. If anyone reads it,
it is my gift for them to unpack within, understand

its meanings and glean the concepts, follow
the breadcrumbs, and arrows pointing to them — we are

the same. My work has already been done — it is
done in the sitting, it happens in the moment of re-cognition,

it is the salt in the tears of letting go, undoing and untangling
the lies. It is done in the new sight, of *living what is* — the writing

of it is the loving report to a world pained by its own captivating
bling. Freedom is not a symbol on a flag or by a vote solely,

or to claim the right to inflict harm upon another,
freedom comes by saying 'no' to what is not real.

All-ness

My heart full, feeling
no-thing-ness, unimportance:
belonging to All.

Acknowledgements & Gratitude

My friends, Christa, Ananda and Ananda Group, Mimi, Spike, Monique, Genny, Vallerie, Gloria, my late parents, Mark, Ramsey, Eli, Jeff, Phelgaye, Bill, Alystyre, Richard, Randy, Jim and car, Anna Lee, Mary Tyler, Jenita, Sharon Graff, Phillip and Woodstock Poetry Society, ACAT, Dr. Yeo and ACA, Liz, TTC and Cooper Square, Tenement neighbors, PUI and pandemic response, Anna, Salma's, Elizabeth St. Garden and McNally Jackson, Bob Krasner Photography, Nathan and Think Coffee, Alex Fatouros, Kelly N. Ellis, NYC, NYC Parks Dept., NYC public library, and 311, my Alexander Technique students, and the staff at Atmosphere Press.

About Atmosphere Press

Atmosphere Press is an independent, full-service publisher for excellent books in all genres and for all audiences. Learn more about what we do at atmospherepress.com.

We encourage you to check out some of Atmosphere's latest releases, which are available at Amazon.com and via order from your local bookstore:

Melody in Exile, by S.T. Grant

Covenant, by Kate Carter

Near Scattered Praise Lies Our Substantial Endeavor, by Ron Penoyer

Weightless, Woven Words, by Umar Siddiqui

Journeying: Flying, Family, Foraging, by Nicholas Ranson

Lexicon of the Body, by DM Wallace

Controlling Chaos, by Michael Estabrook

Almost a Memoir, by M.C. Rydel

Throwing the Bones, by Caitlin Jackson

Like Fire and Ice, by Eli

Sway, by Tricia Johnson

A Patient Hunger, by Skip Renker

Lies of an Indispensable Nation: Poems About the American Invasions of Iraq and Afghanistan, by Lilvia Soto

The Carcass Undressed, by Linda Eguiliz

Poems That Wrote Me, by Karissa Whitson

Gnostic Triptych, by Elder Gideon

For the Moment, by Charnjit Gill

Battle Cry, by Jennifer Sara Widelitz

I woke up to words today, by Daniella Deutsch

Never Enough, by William Guest

Second Adolescence, by Joe Rolnicki

About the Author

Cate McNider is a multi-disciplinary artist and a certified psycho-physical practitioner and movement educator registered as The Listening Body®. Since arriving in NYC in 1985, she has expressed her healing journey through poetry, multimedia movement performances, and painting. She has performed her multimedia works in downtown venues and Brooklyn, and exhibited her paintings in solo shows in the East Village and NOHO. Poems from her first collection, *Separation and Return*, have been in several journals, in print and online. *Escape Velocity* is the follow up on the success of her healing practices. Cate still lives in New York.